D1520690

Summary

Of

The Plant Paradox:

The Hidden Dangers in "Healthy" Foods That Cause Disease and Weight Gain

By

Dr Steven Gundry

Copyright © 2017 Concise Reading

All rights reserved.

ISBN:

9781976726392

DEDICATION

For everyone who loves reading and books.

Whenever you read a good book, somewhere in the world a door opens to allow in more light. —Vera Nazarian

Table of Contents

Attention: Our Free Gift To You

As a way to say "Thank You" for being a fan of our series, we have included a free gift for you.

To get your free gift, please visit:

http://www.concisereading.com/gift/

The Concise Reading Team

Disclaimer

Note to readers:
This is an unofficial summary & analysis of Dr Steven Gundry's "The Plant Paradox: The Hidden Dangers in "Healthy" Foods That Cause Disease and Weight Gain" designed to enrich your reading experience.

Disclaimer: All Rights Reserved. No part of this publication may be reproduced or retransmitted, electronic or mechanical, without the written permission of the publisher; with the exception of brief quotes used in connection in reviews written for inclusion in a magazine or newspaper.

This Book is licensed for your personal enjoyment only. This Book may not be re-sold or given away to other people. If you would like to share this book with another person, please purchase an additional copy for each recipient. If you're reading this book and did not purchase it, please purchase your own copy.

Product names, logos, brands, and other trademarks featured or referred to within this publication are the property of their respective trademark holders. These trademark holders are not affiliated with us and they do not sponsor or endorse our publications. This book is unofficial and unauthorized. It is not authorized, approved, licensed, or endorsed by the aforementioned interests or any of their licensees.

The information in this book has been provided for educational and entertainment purposes only.

The information contained in this book has been compiled from sources deemed reliable and it is accurate to the best of the Author's knowledge; however, the Author cannot guarantee its accuracy and validity and cannot be held liable for any errors or omissions. Upon using the information contained in this book, you agree to hold harmless the Author from and against any damages, costs, and expenses, including any legal fees, potentially resulting from the application of any of the information provided by this guide. The disclaimer applies to any damages or injury caused by the use and application, whether directly or indirectly, of any advice or information presented, whether for breach of contract, tort, neglect, personal injury, criminal intent, or under any other cause of action. You agree to accept all risks of using the information presented inside this book.

The fact that an individual or organization is referred to in this document as a citation or source of information does not imply that the author or publisher endorses the information that the individual or organization provided. This is an unofficial summary & analytical review and has not been approved by the original author of the book.

Summary of The Plant Paradox

INTRODUCTION

In the book's introduction, Dr Gundry sheds some light on the autobiographical inspiration behind *The Plant Paradox*. He once struggled with being overweight, having high blood pressure, migraines, headaches, high cholesterol levels, arthritis and insulin resistance. After successfully fighting his way back into good health, he aims to help readers in similar situations to improve their health. His advice claims to combat the group of diseases that have become widespread in developed nations since the 1960s: "obesity, type 1 and type 2 diabetes, autoimmune diseases, asthma, allergies and sinus conditions, arthritis, cancer, heart disease, osteoporosis, Parkinson's disease, and dementia". He also reveals that he left his prestigious position as professor of surgery and pediatrics in cardiothoracic surgery and head of cardiothoracic surgery at Loma Linda University School of Medicine (one he held for sixteen years) because he was convinced that he could "reverse heart disease with diet instead of surgery". His background as a physician, cardiologist, heart disease expert and immunologist has allowed him to provide a new and promising perspective on the perennial question of what we should eat, and in what amounts.

He does not disagree with experts who point towards the increasingly sedentary lives we lead, the popularity of fast food and drinks spiked with high-fructose corn syrup, and an environment filled with toxins as contributing factors to our host of contemporary health ailments. However, he argues that a "common cause" for many of these health problems has been overlooked by health experts, scientists and journalists. This is the existence of lectins, plant proteins that are often found in plant seeds, which serve to protect them from unwanted predation from insects and mammals (including humans). The book's title thus alludes to the paradox that plant consumption can be both beneficial and harmful (one should thus be able to differentiate between them) and that some plants should only be consumed in small and moderate amounts.

After introducing the book's mission statement, he delineates its structure. Part I presents the scientific explanation of how plants can have both positive and negative effects on human health. Part II outlines the three-day cleanse that readers should undertake before embarking on the Plant Paradox Program, as well as its dietary prescriptions (his "blueprint for longevity") that readers should adhere to in the long term for optimal health. Part III consists of suggested meal plans and recipes.

PART I: The Dietary Dilemma

CHAPTER 1: The War Between Plants and Animals

The book's first chapter outlines the evolutionary biology of the plant kingdom in an accessible way. Dr Gundry mainly focuses on two evolutionary pressures which have shaped the biochemical properties of most plants:

(1) the need to deter and discourage predators through the use of camouflage, toxins, resins, saps, poisons, bitter-tasting tannins and alkaloids, protective structures, etc.;

(2) the need to entice animals, birds and insects to help transport plant seeds and spores over a wider territory.

He makes it clear that humans need to consume plants to access the "hundreds of vitamins, minerals, antioxidants, and other nutrients" required for excellent health. However, we need to be more discerning over the types of plants we incorporate into our everyday diet, as well as the quantities in which we consume them.

There is an ample focus on lectins, which play a major role among the plant kingdom's repertoire of defensive strategies and has a potent ability to harm human health. Gluten is the most infamous lectin, which are plant proteins that serve to discourage insects and mammals from consuming the plants that produce them in the future. They have the ability to

(1) bind to sugar molecules on our cells, triggering inflammatory responses and disrupting intercellular communication;
(2) stimulate weight gain;
(3) confuse the immune system with molecular mimicry;
(4) cause severe heartburn and pain to the livestock that consume corn and soy, and cause secondary harm to the humans who consume their meat, milk and egg products.

Humans have also developed various lines of defense to minimize the negative impact caused by lectins; individuals which have any of these defense mechanisms compromised stand to suffer from more adverse health consequences.

CHAPTER 2: *Lectins on the Loose*

The book's second chapter aims to address this "obvious" question: "If our forebears have been eating most of these lectin-containing foods for thousands of years, why are they only now undermining our health?"

Dr Gundry explains that several key events in human civilization have worked in tandem to cause this:

(1) the invention of fire, which allowed humans to consume a wider range of plant species;

(2) the cultivation of grains and legumes during the agricultural revolution;

(3) a spontaneous mutation in Northern European cows that caused them to produce the protein casein A-1 (which prompts an immune attack on the pancreas when consumed - in their milk) instead of the normal casein A-2;

(4) the importing of New World foods to Europe when Columbus discovered the Americas;

(5) the introduction of genetically modified organisms (GMOs).

The fast and unprecedented speed in which these various developments occurred has outpaced the ability of the human microbiome (the gut bacteria that helps us digest food and protects us from its harmful components) to effectively adapt to them. Ancient civilizations may have benefited from the extended lifespans afforded by agriculture, which reduced the risks of starvation, but they also had to cope with the adverse health effects caused by lectin consumption. Furthermore, the popularity of processed foods which contain lectin-rich corn, soy and wheat and the advent of herbicides, biocides, drugs, fertilizers, food additives, skin-care products and other chemicals have increased our lectin loads and compromised our ability to cope with them.

Dr Gundry then argues that a gluten-free diet does not reduce one's exposure to lectins. When people avoid wheat, barley, rye and oats to eliminate gluten from their diets, they turn to gluten-free products which contain lectins in the form of flour derived from grains and pseudo-grains. Unfortunately, many of these other lectins that triggers celiac disease, brain fog, joint pain and inflammation in those who are gluten-sensitive and lead to more detrimental health effects than gluten. Therefore, he observed that many of his patients suffered from digestive and health problems (including weight issues) despite eliminating barley, rye, oats, and wheat (BROW) from their diets. The negative health effects of grain consumption are compounded by their use as livestock feed, as well as the over-use of antibiotics in the livestock industry.

Dr Gundry then describes how lectins can trigger an "immunologic and hormonal firestorm" in our bodies by mimicking the protein surfaces of harmful bacteria, and thus cause an unwarranted full-scale inflammatory immunological response. After listing a 49 different ailments caused by lectin (from acne to vitiligo), he concludes that "Very small things (like lectins) can cause huge health problems".

CHAPTER 3: Your Gut Under Attack

The holobiome is the central focus of this chapter. It constitutes not only the microbiome (the microbes in our gut), but also the microbes on our skin and the "cloud of bacteria" that envelopes all of us. The holobiome consists of trillions of bacteria, beneficial viruses, molds, fungi, protozoa and even worms, and constitutes 90% of all our cells and 99% of the genetic material within our bodies. The Human Microbiome Project has only identified over ten thousand distinct organisms in our holobiome thus far.

Dr Gundry explains that the beneficial microbes in our intestines play a crucial role in breaking down and digesting the cell walls of the plants we consume, allowing us to extract energy and nutrients from our food. This can only happen when they work in tandem with the acids and enzymes in our digestive system, breaking down food into its constituent amino acids, fatty acids and sugar molecules that can be absorbed into the bloodstream through our intestinal walls. Our mutually symbiotic with our holobiome is also crucial for the optimal functioning of our immune system, nervous system, and hormonal system.

Unfortunately, the confluence of various factors in our modern environments has disrupted the healthy functioning of our holobiome. Lectins cause major inflammatory responses when they breach the intestinal mucosal border, allowing other larger molecules to pass through while blocking the absorption of smaller nutrients and vitamins. Furthermore, the increased consumption of over-the-counter painkillers – particularly nonsteroidal anti-inflammatory drugs (NSAIDs) such as Advil and Motrin, ibuprofen, Aleve, Naprosyn, Mobic, Celebrex, and aspirin – has further compromised our mucus-lined intestinal barrier. Lectins, bacteria, and lipopolysaccharides (LPSs) can thus invade our body, causing inflammation and pain when our immune system reacts to them.

To maintain good health, we must create conditions that allow for good microbes to thrive in our guts and maintain the integrity of the intestinal border.

CHAPTER 4: Know Thy Enemy:

The Seven Deadly Disruptors

Chapter four begins with a description of an "infamous experiment". When a frog is dropped into a pot of boiling water, it immediately leaps out. When dropped into a pot of lukewarm water which is slowly brought to boil, however, it does not register the temperature rise and "blissfully boils to death". Likewise, Dr Gundry argues that we have failed to register the subtle changes that have collectively caused a disastrous effect on our health. While many public policy experts will point towards an increasing life expectancy as proof of better health, he notes that this statistical increase can actually be attributed to the reductions of deaths from infectious diseases (such as measles, German measles, mumps, diphtheria, typhoid fever, scarlet fever, whooping cough, and influenza) which disproportionally impacted infants and children. This increase in average life expectancies can thus mostly be attributed to the use of vaccines and antibiotics, as well as reduced infant mortality rates via better prenatal care and childbirth practice. Improve life expectancy does not automatically guarantee improved health expectancy.

Most of the chapter is taken up by an elaboration of the seven deadly and subtle changes which have drastically altered our health expectancies:

(1) the widespread use of broad-spectrum antibiotics to treat bacterial infections in humans and livestock, indiscriminately killing both good and bad gut bacteria;

(2) the consumption of Nonsteroidal Anti-Inflammatory Drugs (NSAIDs), damages the mucosal barrier in the small intestine and colon;

(3) the consumption of stomach-acid blockers such as Zantac, Prilosec, Nexium, and Protonix, allows bad bacteria to flourish;

(4) the introduction of artificial sweeteners causes weight gain because brain has been tricked by the sweetness;

(5) the prevalence of endocrine disruptors in the form of chemicals found in most plastics, such as scented cosmetics, mouthwash, deodorants, antiperspirants, hand sanitizers, food preservatives, sunscreens, and even cash register receipts, all of which destroy good bacteria and trigger hormonal irregularities;

(6) the adoption of genetically modified foods (GMO) and the herbicide Roundup in American agriculture, negatively affects the composition of your gut flora;

(7) the constant exposure to blue light from televisions, cell phones, tablets, and other electronic devices, disrupts your circadian rhythms.

Healthy substitutes for several harmful pain-relieving drugs, acid-reducer drugs, sleep-aid drugs and the various endocrine-disrupting chemicals are provided. For example, one should

.ute plastic wrap and plastic bags with old-fashioned wax paper .eusable cloth sandwich bags. GMO food products should be .ibstituted with organic food, while blue light can be avoided via apps (for example – justgetflux.com) and blue light-blocking glasses.

CHAPTER 5: How the Modern Diet Makes You Fat

(and Sick)

Early on in this chapter, Dr Gundry announces his intention to help us live by Hippocrates' famous declaration: "Let food be thy medicine and medicine be thy food." Before his dietary prescriptions are introduced, however, he provides an overview of how our agricultural history has lead up to the present status quo, where the rate of obesity, diabetes, asthma, arthritis, cancer, heart disease, osteoporosis, Parkinson's disease, and dementia has skyrocketed. The usual factors deemed responsible for this phenomenon (such as calorie-rich Western diets, pollution in the environment, sedentary lifestyles, greater BMIs) certainly play a part, but there is a case to be made for why our increased lectin consumption has played a major but mostly invisible role (until now).

Before the advent of agriculture, humans lived a nomadic hunter-gatherer lifestyle across the globe. Their diet primarily consisted of seasonal fruits, seasonal big game, fish, shellfish and starches in the form of plant tubers (which were roasted once fire was discovered 100,000 years ago). Settled agriculture introduced human reliance on grains, beans, and milk as primary food sources, since all three could be harvested and stored for long term periods as a form of insurance against bad weather, crop destruction by pests or the winter months. Furthermore, these foods can "literally

.rge fat storage" for any given calorie relative to other food

cts – and were thus essential when starvation was a threat. This

.rs because lectin

(1) encourages the conversion of sugar to fat;

(2) blocks muscle cells from utilizing glucose, which is directed instead to fat cells;

(3) blocks sugar from entering the brain, thus creating feelings of hunger and prompting increased food consumption.

The rapid weight gain via consumption of the lectins in grains and beans was once crucial to survival (in anticipation of winter and other food-scarce periods), but has now become a liability.

Dr Gundry then moves on the assess the efficacy of low-carb diets (South Beach, Atkins and Paleo), and argues that any weight loss or improved health experienced from adhering to them was *not* due to the restriction of carbohydrates or the increased consumption of protein and fat. Instead, the positive changes were gained from the elimination of lectin-rich foods. The same principle holds true for ketogenic diets (which restrict both protein and carbohydrates) and low-fat, whole-grain diets. He also argues that the beneficial health effects obtained from the elimination of red meat from our diets were caused by the genetic mutation of a lectin-attracting sugar molecule - Neu5Ac (which is nearly identical to the Neu5Gc found it cattle, pigs, and sheep) in our bodies. We thus stand to benefit from reducing our animal protein intake (especially of chicken, beef, mutton and pork which have been feed lectin-rich soy and corn).

PART II: Introducing

the Plant Paradox Program

CHAPTER 6: Revamp Your Habits

After explaining the science behind the Plant Paradox Program, Dr Gundry proceeds to outline its rules, guidelines and prescriptions.

He lists four main rules that govern the program:

(1) what you stop eating is more important than what you start eating;

(2) be sure to care and nourish healthy gut bacteria;

(3) "Fruit might as well be candy" (with the exception of unripe bananas, avocados, mangoes and papayas): Dr Gundry points out that even food items that are typically considered to be vegetables (zucchini, tomatoes, bell peppers, eggplant, pickle) are botanically fruits if they contain seeds. All fruits are to be avoided because they emit signals to the brain to store fat for the winter when consumed;

(4) "You are what the thing you are eating, ate": Dr Gundry notes that most of the food and drink items popularized by the fast food industry are derived from corn in one form or another, such

as corn oil, corn starch, cornmeal, corn syrup, and corn feed for chickens, pigs and cows.

Chapter 6 also includes an outline of the three phases within the Plant Paradox Program.

(1) Phase 1 involves a three-day cleanse that aims to alter the balance between the good and bad microorganisms in your gut. This phase will be discussed in further details in Chapter 7.

(2) Phase 2 consists of a two-week long adherence to new eating habits. This involves:

- The elimination of grains, legumes, GMO foods, sugars, saturated fats, artificial sweeteners, and industrial farm-raised poultry.

- Moderate amounts of omega-3 fats (via fish oil, perilla oil, or flaxseed oil), animal protein (seafood and eggs/meat from pastured or omega-3-fed chickens, grass-fed or pasture-raised beef or pork) and ghee.

- Minimal intake of dairy products from the breeds of cows, sheep or goats that produce casein A-2.

(3) Phase 3 involves intermittent fasting and the reduction of animal protein intake (including fish) to a total of 2-4 ounces per day. The excluded foods from Phase 2 can be slowly re-introduced in moderate amounts if your body does not demonstrate a negative reaction to them. The Keto Plant Paradox Intensive Care

Program is introduced for patients who are suffering from other diseases such as kidney disease and diabetes.

Dr Gundry closes the chapter by reiterating that the diet is crucial even for those who are already athletic and lean. He argues that it can be adhered to without a deep understanding of human metabolism and nutrition (one can simply adhere to its prescriptions without comprehending the scientific explanations), and that no one is ever too old to make positive changes in their diet and lifestyle. He ends the chapter by asserting that we are no different from great apes that eat fruit to gain weight for the winter, livestock which are fattened up with grains, corn and beans, and horses which are fattened with oats for the winter.

CHAPTER 7: Phase 1:

Kick-Start with a Three-Day Cleanse

The primary objective of the "Three-Day Kick-Start Cleanse" is to starve all the gut bacteria that are responsible for stimulating immune responses, contributing to weight gain, and to prompt you to crave unhealthy foods in unwarranted quantities. When executed properly, the cleanse can completely alter the ecosystem of bacteria in your gut, paving the way for better digestion and absorption of your new and improved diet in Phase 2. However, this hard-won balance can always be disrupted again when you revert back to your bad habits.

The restrictions during this phase are particularly strict:

(1) no dairy, grains or pseudo-grains, fruit, sugar, seeds, eggs, soy, nightshade plants, roots, or tubers;

(2) no corn, soy, canola, or other inflammatory oils, along with any form of beef or other farm animal meat.

These food items are to be replaced with vegetables and small amounts of fish or pastured chicken (meat-free recipes are available for vegans and vegetarian). You are encouraged to feast on a wide range of vegetables, including all varieties from the cabbage family, lettuce, spinach, Swiss chard, watercress, asparagus, celery, fennel, artichokes, radishes, onions, garlic, leeks, chives, kelp, seaweed and fresh herbs (mint, parsley, basil, and cilantro).

Fats and oil can be obtained from olives, avocados, avocado oil, coconut oil, macadamia nut oil, sesame seed oil, walnut oil, extra-virgin olive oil, hemp seed oil, and flaxseed oil. The quality of the foods you consume is also critical: all vegetables should be 100% organic, all seafood should be wild caught, and all chicken should be pastured.

Dr Gundry also recommends that you clean your gut with an herbal laxative called Swiss Kriss (this is "absolutely optional") and that you augment your cleanse with natural supplements that kill off bad gut bacteria, molds and fungi; for example, Oregon grape root extract, grapefruit seed extract, mushroom extracts, and spices such as black pepper, cloves, cinnamon, and wormwood.

CHAPTER 8: Phase 2: Repair and Restore

Phase 2 lasts for a minimum of six weeks – the amount of time it takes to cement the Plant Paradox Program's new eating habits. Dr Gundry observes that this is likely to be the most challenging part of the program, since you are likely to experience withdrawal symptoms (low energy, headaches, grouchiness, and muscle cramps) as a result of abandoning the foods that used to form the bulk of your diet. The core objective of this phase is to eliminate all the lectin-rich foods that are compromising the integrity of your intestinal linings and triggering inflammatory immune responses in your body.

The chapter includes an extensive list of acceptable foods ("Say Yes Please") and banned foods ("Just Say No"). Some fruits, vegetables and oils are allowed while others are banned, creating an overlap between the food categories.

The list of acceptable foods is grouped into several categories:

(1) oils (mainly vegetable oils, nut oils and cod liver oil);

(2) sweeteners;

(3) nuts and seeds;

(4) olives;

(5) dark chocolate;

(6) vinegars;

(7) herbs and seasonings;

(8) energy bars;

(9) flours;

(10) ice cream;

(11) noodles;

(12) dairy products;

(13) wine;

(14) spirits;

(15) fish;

(16) fruits (berries, avocado, apples, peaches, etc.);

(17) vegetables (mainly cruciferous vegetables and leafy greens);

(18) resistant starches;

(19) pastured poultry;

(20) meat;

(21) plant-based "meats".

The list of excluded foods includes foods that were introduced to the human diet within the past ten thousand years (when crop cultivation began), and are grouped into

(1) refined, starchy foods;

(2) vegetables (which contain high amounts of lectin);

(3) nuts and seeds;

(4) fruits (peppers and fruits that are often considered to be vegetables, for instance tomatoes);

(5) non-Southern European cow's milk products;

(6) grains;

(7) oils (soy, grape seed, sunflower, corn, etc.).

Dr Gundry argues that the human body has not had enough time to develop an immunological tolerance to the crops that were recently introduced, and elaborates on how whole grains, beans, peas, soybeans, lentils, eggplants, potatoes, peppers, pumpkin, zucchinis, goji berries, tomatoes, squash, peanuts, cashews, sunflower seeds, chia seeds, pumpkin seeds, corn (maize), and quinoa should be avoided because they contain large amounts of lectin.

The chapter includes additional prescriptions to avoid stomach-acid-blocking drugs and NSAIDs, along with recommendations to consume fish oil supplements, vitamin D supplements, probiotics, and other targeted supplements.

When you begin to see the positive effects of sticking to the program – normal weight, the alleviation of aches and pains, the clearing of brain fog, the dissipating of gut issues and autoimmune symptoms – it is time to proceed to the next phase.

CHAPTER 9: Phase 3: Reap the Rewards

Dr Gundry compares Phase 3 of the Plant Paradox Program to a harvest, where you get to reap the benefits of a healthy and symbiotic relationship with your holobiome. At this point, you should benefit from greater energy levels, a healthy weight, and improved long-term health prospects. In addition, you should have regained a healthy ecosystem of gut bacteria, an appropriate weight, normal bowel movements, pain-free joints, improved skin, and more energy. Certain lectins may now be reintroduced and consumed regularly again if your body proves to be capable of coping with them now.

In Phase 3, you are advised to continue eating the recommended foods and avoiding the excluded ones. However, greater amounts of ketogenic fats, immature lectin-bearing foods (e. g. cucumbers, zucchini, Japanese eggplant, tomatoes, and peppers), pressure-cooked legumes, and Indian white basmati rice can be slowly reintroduced into your diet in small and moderate amounts. Dr Gundry recommends intermittent fasting and reduced food/calorie consumption (especially animal protein).

He then segues to an overview of Dan Buettner's bestselling book *The Blue Zones*, which describes the food cultures of the regions of the world which have proven to be the most conducive to human longevity: "the Italian island of Sardinia; Okinawa, Japan; Loma Linda, California; the Nicoya Peninsula of Costa Rica; and the Greek island of Ikaria". He points out that all of these cultures consume only small amounts of animal protein (particularly seafood), and recommends that you emulate them. He also cites his own experience in testing the levels of insulin-like growth factor 1 (IGF-1) in his patients' blood. The results show that IGF-1 is positively correlated with the risk of developing cancer; and lower IGF-1 levels were associated with reduced sugar and animal protein consumption.

CHAPTER 10: The Keto Plant Paradox

Intensive Care Program

Dr Gundry explains how the mitochondria is responsible for using sugars and fats to produce the energy-generating ATP molecules required for cellular function. At night, they turn to fats (in the form of ketones) as a source of energy when sugar and protein supplies are low. A similar cycle occurs between the summer and winter months, since fats and sugars were historically unavailable during the winter. In modern environments, however, our bodies perpetually produce insulin to direct sugar to the mitochondria and to convert them into fat for future use. Without your body experiencing lower levels of sugar and protein consumption (as animal protein consumption also facilitates high insulin levels), the opportunity to convert the stored fats to energy never emerges.

Given these biochemical connections, Dr Gundry argues that the elimination of lectins, fruits and unwarranted amounts of animal protein will help stave off insulin resistance, diabetes and kidney diseases – since ketones "burn cleaner" than protein. He then introduces the kidney-friendly Keto Plant Paradox Intensive Care Program, which calls for greater reductions in animal protein, fruit and seeded vegetable consumption. The stringent program is meant for those facing other critical health issues such as cancer, kidney disease, dementia, diabetes, Parkinson's disease and Alzheimer's.

CHAPTER 11: Plant Paradox

Supplement Recommendations

Dr Gundry cites a 1936 document from the U. S. Senate stating that "foods—fruits, vegetables and grains—now being raised on millions of acres of land that no longer contains enough of certain needed nutrients, are starving us—no matter how much we eat of them". This report is used to support his claim that nutrient supplementation is a critical component of the Plant Paradox Program. The quality of the nutrition we gain from modern agriculture has been compromised by the use of petrochemical fertilizers, pesticides, biocides, and Roundup. Furthermore, our hunter-gatherer ancestors once benefited from access to 250 different plants on a rotating and seasonal basis, each enriched by access to bacteria and fungi deep in the soil.

He therefore recommends that you consume various nutritional supplements to compensate for modern micronutritient deficits: vitamin D, vitamin B (especially methyl-folate and methylcobalamin), polyphenols, green plant phytochemicals, prebiotics, lectin blockers, "sugar defence", and long-chain omega-3 fatty acids. These supplements will enhance the results of the Plant Paradox Program, but will not be able to act as a substitute to it.

PART III: Meal Plans and Recipes

This part of the book consists of sample meal plans for each phase of the Plant Paradox Program. Three days of meals are outlined for the Three-Day Kick-Start Cleanse, two weeks of meals for Phase 2, and five days of meals for Phase 3. A week's worth of meals is then presented for the Keto Plant Paradox Intensive Care Program.

Dr Gundry then provides the recipes for thirty-six easy-to-prepare dishes, which were created with the help of Catalyst Cuisine's Irina Skoeries. The ingredients which are typically unavailable in supermarkets can be found in natural foods stores, Amazon, Vitacost, Thrive Market and other online retailers. The following cooking tools will be required: a blender, food processor, Magic Bullet, microwave oven, mini food processor, pressure cooker, salad spinner, and spiralizer.

Background Information about

The Plant Paradox

The Plant Paradox was published in April 2017 by Harper Wave, the "health, wellness, lifestyle, and inspirational" division of HarperCollins. Its author, Dr Steven Gundry, M.D. argues that plants are good for us because they contain antioxidants, nutrients and vitamins; meanwhile, plants can also be bad for us due to lectins. He argues that plants have evolved to produce lectin as a means to deter predation, and are responsible for inflammatory responses, digestive problems, heart disease, cancer, weight gain, mental health issues, dementia and other health ailments in humans. Our bodies have different capacities to protect us from the lectins we consume, with some individuals being more adversely affected than others. Gluten, for example, is a type of lectin that is especially harmful to the 1-2% of the population that suffers from celiac disease.

The first part of the book uses evolutionary biology and human agricultural history to explain the science behind how lectin harms us, while the second part presents an overview of the Plant Paradox Program that we should adhere to for optimal health. Besides insisting on reduced animal protein consumption, it also counterintuitively warns against fruits and vegetables that are generally considered to be healthy: lentils, beans, peppers, tomatoes, squashes, cashew nuts, hummus, cucumbers, most fruits (unless they are unripe), quinoa, brown rice and whole grains. Pressure cookers, seed removal and rind peeling are also suggested as a means of removing lectin-filled plant parts.

The book is interspersed with brief case studies that detail how Dr Gundry's dietary advice helped solved various mental and physical health issues (with R&B singer Usher appearing as his most famous client). The third part includes numerous sample meal plans and recipes.

The Plant Paradox was fairly well-received upon publication, but it has its share of detractors among the medical community. James Hamblin, MD, a senior editor at *The Atlantic* noted the conflicts of interest at play (Dr Gundry is selling the very same health supplements he recommends in the program) and pointed out that there was contradictory evidence for lectin consumption being harmful [1]. Thomas Colin Campbell, who is the Jacob Gould Schurman Professor Emeritus of Nutritional Biochemistry at Cornell University and a specialist on the effect of nutrition on long-term health, has pointed out that many of the book's academic references "do not offer any support for the statements he makes in the text or are misrepresented[2]".

---

[1] https://www.theatlantic.com/health/archive/2017/04/the-next-gluten/523686/
[2] http://nutritionstudies.org/the-plant-paradox-by-steven-grundy-md-commentary/

Background Information about

Dr Steven Gundry

Dr Steven R. Gundry earned his medical degree from the Medical College of Georgia in 1977, after graduating from Yale University in 1972. He served as the as professor of surgery and pediatrics in cardiothoracic surgery and head of cardiothoracic surgery at Loma Linda University School of Medicine for sixteen years. He holds patents on a number of medical devices, including the cardiac cannula and a suction retractor[3]. In 2002, he pivoted from his career as a surgeon to focus on dietary health interventions and to study the human microbiome after founding The Center for Restorative Medicine. His Plant Paradox program focuses on eliminating lectins, which he promotes alongside his supplements on gundrymd.com (which aims "dramatically improve human health, happiness, and longevity through [his] unique vision of diet and nutrition").

---

[3] https://patents.justia.com/inventor/steven-r-gundry

Cover Questions

1. What are lectins, and how do they harm you?

2. What commonalities do the societies living in "the blue zones" (regions which are home to the world's longest-lived people) have in terms of diet?

3. What are the "seven deadly disruptors" of our health?

Trivia Questions about

The Plant Paradox

1. Why should we limit our intake of animal protein?

2. Why does Dr Gundry argue that gluten-free products are bad for you?

3. Which type of calorie-rich plant sources does Dr Gundry recommend?

4. Why did plants evolve to produce lectin?

5. Why haven't humans evolved to effectively combat lectin's harmful effects on our bodies?

6. What is the difference between the holobiome and the microbiome?

7. Why does Dr Gundry compare fruits to candy?

8. How can we tip the balance between beneficial and harmful gut bacteria?

Trivia Questions about

Dr Steven Gundry

1. How does Dr Gundry encourage his patients to adhere to all his stringent prescriptions in the Plant Paradox Program?

2. How did Dr Gundry's career as a surgeon prepare him to offer nutritional advice to the public?

3. Besides the book itself, what is Dr Gundry selling to readers?

4. What kind of tests did Dr Gundry perform on his patients to assess the effects of having them adhere to his diet?

5. Do you agree with Dr Gundry's claim that he has discovered the "common cause for most health problems"?

Discussion Questions

1. How would you compare *The Plant Paradox* to other popular books that claim to possess the knowledge of what we should and should not eat?

2. What are some of the changes in modern food production systems that are responsible for our adverse health outcomes?

3. Do you agree that average health expectancies have declined as average life expectancies increased?

4. After reading the book, do you agree with the claim that "lectins are the #1 Biggest Danger in the American Diet"?

5. Were you convinced about the efficacy of the Plant Paradox Program after reading the book? Why or why not?

6. Why are prebiotics and probiotics important?

7. What are some of the negative side effects of antibiotic consumption?

8. Why does Dr Gundry state that "you are what you eat, and what the things you are eating, ate"?

9. What are Dr Gundry's reasons for advising readers to avoid GMOs?

10. Do you think that there is sufficient scientific evidence to equate the consumption of ripe fruits with candy?

Thank You

We hope that you've enjoyed your reading experience.

Here at Concise Reading, we will always strive to deliver to you the highest quality guides.

We'd like to thank you for supporting us and reading until the very end.

Before you go, would you mind leaving us a review on Amazon?

It will mean a lot to us and help us continue to create high quality guides for you in the future.

Warmly yours,

The Concise Reading Team

94888428R00031

Made in the USA
Columbia, SC
02 May 2018